INSIDE COLLEGE
FOOTBALL

TEXAS
LONGHORNS

BY WILLIAM MEIER

SportsZone

An Imprint of Abdo Publishing
abdobooks.com

abdobooks.com

Published by Abdo Publishing, a division of ABDO, PO Box 398166, Minneapolis, Minnesota 55439. Copyright © 2021 by Abdo Consulting Group, Inc. International copyrights reserved in all countries. No part of this book may be reproduced in any form without written permission from the publisher. SportsZone™ is a trademark and logo of Abdo Publishing.

Printed in the United States of America, North Mankato, Minnesota
032020
092020

THIS BOOK CONTAINS
RECYCLED MATERIALS

Cover Photo: David J. Phillip/AP Images
Interior Photos: Kiichiro Sato/AP Images, 5; Bill Nichols/AP Images, 7, 9; Aaron M. Sprecher/AP Images, 11; AP Images, 13, 17, 18, 21, 26, 43; Carl E. Linde/AP Images, 15; Bettmann/Getty Images, 22; Rich Clarkson/Sports Illustrated/Set Number: X19936/Getty Images, 25; Eric Gay/AP Images, 29; George Bridges/AP Images, 31; Harry Cabluck/AP Images, 33, 37; Denis Poroy/AP Images, 35; Butch Dill/AP Images, 40

Editor: Patrick Donnelly
Series Designer: Nikki Nordby

Library of Congress Control Number: 2019954417

Publisher's Cataloging-in-Publication Data

Names: Meier, William, author.
Title: Texas Longhorns / by William Meier.
Description: Minneapolis, Minnesota : Abdo Publishing, 2021 | Series: Inside college football | Includes online resources and index.
Identifiers: ISBN 9781532192500 (lib. bdg.) | ISBN 9781644944714 (pbk.) | ISBN 9781098210403 (ebook)
Subjects: LCSH: Texas Longhorns (Football team)--Juvenile literature. | Universities and colleges--Athletics--Juvenile literature. | American football--Juvenile literature. | College sports--United States--History--Juvenile literature.
Classification: DDC 796.33263--dc23

TABLE OF
CONTENTS

CHAPTER 1

TEXAS-SIZED
COMEBACK

Quarterback Vince Young and the Texas Longhorns had been in the spotlight since before the 2005 season even began. Texas was ranked second in the preseason Associated Press (AP) Poll and was expected to contend for a national title. Young and the Longhorns left no doubt about that, going undefeated during the regular season. They scored 40 or more points in all of those wins but one, a 25–22 win over fourth-ranked Ohio State.

Over in the Pac-10 Conference, the University of Southern California (USC) Trojans were the other marquee team that year. Fans had been waiting for months to see Texas and USC play each other. Now, the two teams would finally meet in the Rose Bowl— with the national championship on the line.

The Trojans had won back-to-back national titles in the two years prior. They were in the midst of a 34-game winning streak.

Texas wide receiver Limas Sweed catches a touchdown pass in the Longhorns' 2005 win over Ohio State.

Many people believed the Trojans were one of the best teams of all time. They featured a backfield of senior quarterback Matt Leinart and junior running backs Reggie Bush and LenDale White. Leinart won the Heisman Trophy in 2004 as the nation's top college player. And Bush was the Heisman winner in 2005.

But many thought the Texas quarterback deserved the award. Young, who finished second to Bush in the Heisman voting, was a dynamic player. He proved to be the difference in many games that year. He was a fast and elusive runner. He also threw the ball well. He did all of those things against USC in the Rose Bowl.

Young had to be at his best to lead the kind of comeback Texas needed. The Longhorns' defense had trouble stopping the Trojans all night. Because of that, Texas trailed 38–26 with 6:42 remaining in the game. But Young led the Longhorns down the field and scored on a 17-yard run. The extra point made it 38–33 with 4:03 remaining.

It still looked like the Trojans were going to win, though. USC drove to the Texas 45-yard line with 2:13 left in the game. It was fourth down. All USC needed was two yards to keep the drive going and run out the clock. The Trojans had scored on all four of their possessions in the second half. So USC coach Pete Carroll decided to go for the first down instead of punting.

Leinart took the snap and handed the ball to White, who tried to run up the middle. The Longhorns sent every defender toward the line of scrimmage. There they ran into White and stopped him short of the first down. The Texas defense had finally stopped USC.

Texas quarterback Vince Young eludes USC tacklers during the 2006 Rose Bowl.

Texas took control of the ball with a little more than two minutes remaining. Young then guided the Longhorns to the USC 8-yard line. The Longhorns trailed by five with 26 seconds left in the game. Young stood five yards behind center waiting for the snap. He needed five yards to convert on fourth down.

During his three-year career at Texas, Vince Young did just about everything a player could do. He led the Longhorns to a perfect 13–0 record in 2005 to win the national title. He won the Maxwell Award as the nation's top player. He won the Davey O'Brien Award as the nation's top quarterback. But he fell just short of winning the Heisman Trophy, finishing second to Reggie Bush of USC.

Taking the snap, Young looked into the end zone for an open receiver. Many in the crowd of 93,986 held their breath, waiting for him to throw. Instead, Young saw an opening around the right side. He pulled down the ball and eluded one USC defender behind the line of scrimmage. He then outran another defender into the right corner of the end zone for the go-ahead touchdown.

Young then scored on a two-point conversion to stretch the lead to 41–38 with 19 seconds left. USC didn't have time to counter. Texas held on to win its first national title since 1970.

Young's touchdown run was an exclamation point on an outstanding night. He finished the game with 267 passing yards and completed 30 of his 40 passing attempts. He also rushed for 200 yards on 19 carries.

Young was voted the Most Valuable Player (MVP) of the game, but he was not the only star for the Longhorns. Running backs Selvin Young and Ramonce Taylor combined for 57 rushing yards and two touchdowns. Senior tight end David Thomas caught 10 passes for

Young slips between two USC defenders to score the game-winning touchdown in Texas's 2006 national championship victory over USC.

88 yards. And wide receiver Limas Sweed added eight receptions for 65 yards.

The game would be the final one for Young as a Longhorn. He decided to enter the National Football League (NFL) Draft a few weeks later. But Texas fans will always remember what he did against USC in the Rose Bowl on January 4, 2006.

CHAPTER 2

THE BEGINNINGS OF A POWERHOUSE

On November 30, 1893—Thanksgiving Day—the University of Texas football team played its first game. The players traveled from Austin, Texas, to Dallas, Texas, to face the Dallas Football Club. Dallas was expected to win. But Texas was a surprise winner, 18–16. Approximately 2,000 fans watched the game.

The win started a tradition of success at Texas. Inspired by the victory over Dallas, the team quickly scheduled three more games for the season. Texas defeated a team from San Antonio, Texas, twice and then again faced Dallas. Texas once again prevailed, this time 16–0.

Texas played Texas A&M for the first time on October 19, 1894. Texas cruised to a 38–0 victory. Those teams would go on to become fierce rivals, playing every year from 1915 to 2011, when Texas A&M left the Big 12 Conference.

Texas played football for 10 years before becoming known as the Longhorns.

STORY OF THE LONGHORN

When Texas first started playing football in 1893, the team was called "the Varsity." It was a nickname that lasted for 10 years. In 1904, a sportswriter for the school newspaper, the *Daily Texan*, used the nickname "Longhorns" when he referred to the football team. The use of the nickname stuck, but it was not until 1916 that the longhorn steer became the university's official mascot.

Texas lost only one game in its first three seasons. In fact, the Longhorns did not suffer a losing season until 1933. From 1893 to 1910, Texas won 102 games while losing only 31 and tying seven.

While Texas won year after year, it was rare for a coach to last more than two or three seasons. That is, until Dave Allerdice took over in 1911. He compiled a 33–7 record in five seasons as coach.

Allerdice left after the 1915 season because he did not like the pressure of coaching the Longhorns. Texas then went through two coaches before Berry Whitaker took over in 1920. He established Texas as a football power. In his first season, Texas finished 9–0 overall and 5–0 in Southwest Conference (SWC) play. Texas was nearly as successful the next two seasons. The Longhorns went 6–1–1 in 1921 and 7–2 in 1922. But Whitaker decided to step down after the 1922 season. He also claimed the stress of coaching was too much to handle.

The success on the field continued under coaches E. J. Stewart and Clyde Littlefield. In four seasons as coach, Stewart guided Texas to a 24–9–3 record. Littlefield then took over in 1927. During his

Dana X. Bible watches from the sidelines during a 1946 game against Texas A&M. It was his final season as coach of Texas.

seven years as coach, Texas won two SWC titles and went 44–18–16. But in 1937, Texas was again looking for a new coach. It found the perfect one in Dana X. Bible. He had previously led Texas A&M and Nebraska to a combined 11 conference titles.

Texas won only three games during Bible's first two years as coach. But the team improved to 5–4 in 1939. A 14–13 victory over Arkansas was a turning point for the program. With the game nearly

THE IMPOSSIBLE CATCH

On November 28, 1940, the Longhorns faced Texas A&M in their traditional Thanksgiving showdown. On the third play of the game, Texas junior back Noble Doss hauled in an over-the-shoulder pass reception—a play known as the "impossible catch." Junior fullback Pete Layden then scored on a 1-yard run as Texas defeated A&M 7–0. That broke the Aggies' 19-game winning streak.

over, sophomore running back Jack Crain caught a short pass and raced 67 yards for a touchdown. Crain then kicked the extra point for the win.

In 1941 the Longhorns reached the number-one ranking in the AP Poll. That was the first time the team had ever been the top-ranked team in the country. Texas finished the season ranked fourth in the final AP Poll with an 8–1–1 record. The 1945 team was the first Texas squad to win 10 games.

Bible decided to retire after the 1946 season. He finished his career at Texas with a 63–31–3 record and three conference titles. He also went 2–0–1 in three Cotton Bowl appearances. In 1941 the Cotton Bowl began featuring the winner of the SWC each year. On January 1, 1943, Bible took Texas to its first of many Cotton Bowls. It was also the school's first bowl game appearance.

Blair Cherry, a member of Bible's coaching staff since 1937, took over as coach. Quarterback Bobby Layne, a senior All-American, led the Longhorns to a 10–1 record in 1947. They beat sixth-ranked Alabama 27–7 in the Sugar Bowl. The Sugar Bowl is one of the most prestigious bowl games. Texas finished the year ranked fifth.

Texas beat Georgia Tech 14–7 in the Cotton Bowl on January 1, 1943. It was the first of many Texas appearances in the game.

Texas finished 7–3–1 the following season and defeated number eight Georgia in the Orange Bowl. The Orange Bowl is also an important bowl game. In 1950 the Longhorns went 9–2 overall and a perfect 6–0 in conference play to win the title.

They finished the year ranked third in the AP Poll and second in the United Press International (UPI) coaches' poll. The season ended with a loss to fourth-ranked Tennessee in the Cotton Bowl. It was Cherry's last game. He retired to enter the oil business. Cherry ended his career with a 32–10–1 record.

Ed Price took over the program in 1951 and picked up where Cherry left off. In his first three seasons, the Longhorns won two conference titles and the 1953 Cotton Bowl. But the Longhorns were just a combined 10–19–1 in his final three years. Price resigned after the 1956 season. The Longhorns' next coach would usher in a glorious era of Texas football.

CHAPTER 3

AN ERA OF
CHAMPIONS

The history of Texas was changed forever in December 1956 when the team hired Darrell Royal to be its new coach. At age 32, Royal was one of the youngest coaches in college football. But he turned the Longhorns into a national power.

In his first season, Royal led the team to a 6–4–1 record, a berth in the Sugar Bowl, and a final ranking of eleventh in the AP Poll. Running back James Saxton was Royal's first standout player. Saxton finished third in the Heisman Trophy voting in 1961 as a senior. That year, he led the team to a 10–1 record and a No. 3 ranking in the national polls.

The Longhorns finished the season ranked outside the top 20 in the AP Poll just six times during Royal's 20 years in Austin. They finished ranked fifth or better seven times from 1961 to 1970. But what separated Royal from previous Texas coaches was the fact

As a sophomore, linebacker Tommy Nobis helped Texas win its first national championship in 1963.

✕ Texas held Navy's Heisman Trophy–winning quarterback Roger Staubach (12) in check during the 1964 Cotton Bowl.

that he won national titles. The Longhorns won three championships with him.

Thanks in large part to the play of sophomore linebacker/guard Tommy Nobis, Texas won its first national title in 1963. Nobis is considered by many to be the best Longhorns linebacker ever. He was named All-American twice and was a three-time All-SWC player. Nobis was a leader on the team that went 11–0. The defense allowed just 71 points all season. No team scored more than 13 points in a game against Texas that year.

But the road to the title was not easy. Texas was ranked second after starting the season with three impressive wins. The team rose to number one after beating the top-ranked Oklahoma Sooners 28–7. It was a ranking the Longhorns would not lose. Texas finished the regular season undefeated.

Unlike today, voters in various polls like the AP Poll determined the national champion. And the polls were final after the regular season, not the bowl games. That meant the Longhorns were national champions before their Cotton Bowl matchup with No. 2 Navy. That team was led by junior Heisman Trophy–winning quarterback Roger Staubach.

Most expected the game to be close. But the Longhorns dominated from start to finish. Nobis and tackle Scott Appleton kept Staubach on the run all game. And on offense, senior quarterback Duke Carlisle threw for 213 yards and two touchdowns in the 28–6 victory.

1,000 X 3

From 1966 to 1968, Texas running back Chris Gilbert became the first college player ever to rush for at least 1,000 yards in three straight seasons. He might have made it four years in a row, but freshmen were not eligible to play back then. A three-time team MVP, Gilbert finished his career as the school's and the SWC's all-time leading rusher with 3,231 yards.

"I've never seen a team which deserved to be number one more than Texas," Navy coach Wayne Hardin said after the game. "Texas was just the best we've played, that's all. Staubach didn't play as well as usual, but I imagine Texas had a lot to do with that."

Despite losing Carlisle and Appleton, Texas finished 10–1 in 1964. The top-ranked Alabama Crimson Tide were named the national champions that year. But Texas got a chance to face them in the Orange Bowl.

Quarterback Joe Namath led undefeated Alabama. Just like Staubach one year earlier, Namath struggled against Texas. The Longhorns built a 21–7 halftime lead and held on for a 21–17 victory.

The Longhorns went 9–1–1 in 1968. Royal installed a new offense called the wishbone to take advantage of the running skills of senior back Chris Gilbert and junior quarterback James Street. The offense featured a fullback and two halfbacks. The quarterback could hand off to the fullback or one of the halfbacks, or he could keep the ball himself.

Texas started the season 0–1–1 while getting used to the new offense. But a 31–3 win over Oklahoma State started a streak of 30 consecutive wins and back-to-back national titles in 1969 and 1970.

After winning their last nine games in 1968, the Longhorns started the 1969 season ranked fourth in the nation. They took over the top spot in the AP Poll after a 69–7 win over Texas Christian University on November 15. After a 37-point victory over Texas A&M on Thanksgiving Day, the Longhorns faced second-ranked Arkansas on the road.

Texas had won 18 games in a row. Arkansas had won 15 straight games. President Richard Nixon attended the matchup to award the national title to the winning team. The Longhorns trailed 14–8

× President Richard Nixon gives a plaque to Texas coach Darrell Royal after Texas won the 1969 national championship.

midway through the fourth quarter. Facing fourth down and three yards to go from their own 43-yard line, Street threw a 44-yard pass to tight end Randy Peschel for a first down. Two plays later, running back Jim Bertelsen scored on a two-yard run. Kicker Happy Feller added the extra point to give the Longhorns a 15–14 lead they would not give up.

Texas capped its second national title of the decade with a 21–17 win over No. 9 Notre Dame in the Cotton Bowl. It was also the 500th win in the program's history.

The Longhorns claimed their second straight title in 1970 by finishing the regular season 10–0. Texas outscored its foes 412–125

✖ Texas coach Darrell Royal displays the basics of the wishbone offense.

along the way. The UPI Poll was held at the end of the regular season, and Texas earned the top spot. But by then, the final AP Poll had been moved to after the bowl games. So Texas had to beat No. 6 Notre Dame in the Cotton Bowl to finish first in the AP Poll. Unlike the previous season, the Longhorns failed to slow down the Fighting Irish. Notre Dame snapped Texas's 30-game winning streak with a 24–11 victory. Texas had to share national championship honors with Nebraska, which finished first in the AP Poll.

The Longhorns won three more SWC titles from 1971 to 1973. They ran their streak of consecutive Cotton Bowl appearances to six. But Texas struggled in 1974. The team failed to win the conference

GAME-CHANGING OFFENSE

After the 1967 season, coach Darrell Royal asked assistant Emory Bellard to come up with an offense that would have a lead blocker and take advantage of the team's talented runners. Bellard came up with what is today called the wishbone offense. It features the quarterback and three running backs in the backfield who line up in a "Y," or "wishbone," formation.

Unveiling the new offense in 1968, Texas tied its first game and then lost its second. The Longhorns then won 30 straight games and back-to-back titles thanks to the wishbone. Several of the best team rushing seasons in Texas history came between 1968 and 1976, when the Longhorns featured the formation.

title for the first time since 1967. The Longhorns bounced back to finish 10–2 and win a share of the SWC title in 1975. But they dropped to 5–5–1 in 1976.

Royal retired after that season. He never suffered a losing season in his 20 years at Texas. The Longhorns went 167–47–5 during his tenure and were 109–27–2 in SWC games. Texas won three national titles and 11 conference titles, and the Longhorns appeared in 16 bowl games under Royal. Fans now expected national championships. Those high expectations set the bar for future Texas coaches.

CHAPTER 4

FALLING SHORT AGAIN, AND AGAIN

The retirement of Darrell Royal left a void in the Texas program. Wyoming head coach Fred Akers was given the first chance to fill it. He had spent time as an assistant coach on Royal's staff. Akers quickly showed he would do things his way when he took over in 1977. He switched his offense to the "I" formation to take advantage of the talents of senior running back Earl Campbell.

Campbell had two productive seasons under Royal. As a freshman in 1974, Campbell started at fullback in the wishbone offense and rushed for 928 yards and six touchdowns. As a sophomore, he rushed for 1,118 yards and 13 touchdowns and earned All-America honors. Injuries derailed Campbell's 1976 season. But he was fully healthy in 1977 and produced amazing numbers in Akers's first season as coach.

Texas running back Earl Campbell came back from injury in 1977 to star under new coach Fred Akers.

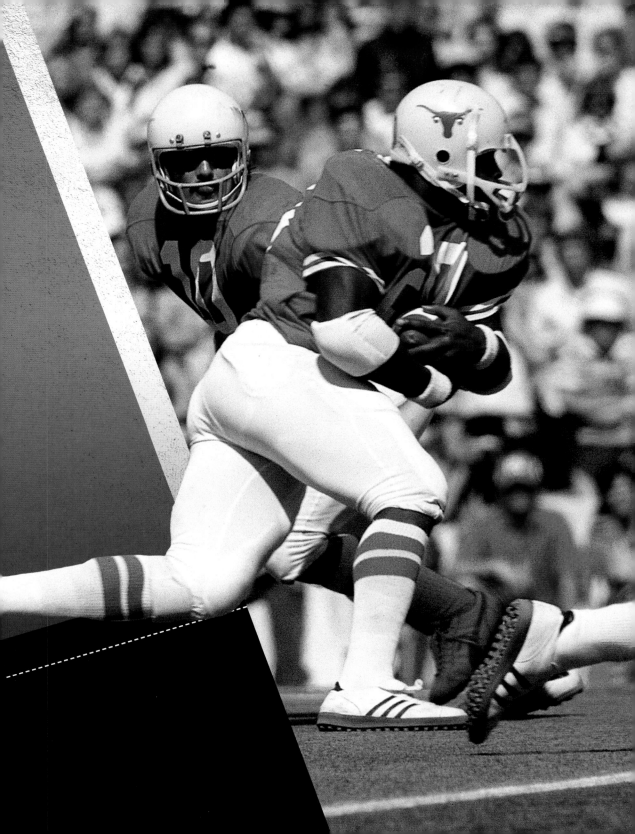

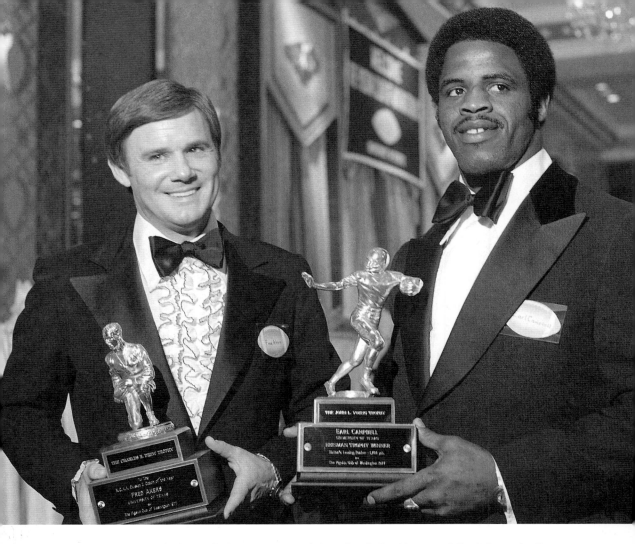

✕ In 1977, Fred Akers, *left*, was named Coach of the Year and Earl Campbell, *right*, won the Heisman Trophy.

Campbell led the Longhorns within one game of the school's fourth national title. He led the nation in rushing with 1,744 yards. That year he topped 100 yards rushing 11 times. He also became the first Texas player to win the Heisman Trophy.

THE TYLER ROSE

Texas great Earl Campbell grew up in Tyler, Texas. He was the sixth of 11 children raised by his mother, Ann. Tyler is known as "the City of Roses" and is home to the Municipal Rose Garden. Because Campbell called Tyler home, he was given the nickname "the Tyler Rose." He became the first Texas player to win the Heisman Trophy in 1977. Campbell led the nation in rushing that year with 1,744 yards. He ended his college career with 4,443 yards. On November 24, 1979, Texas retired his No. 20 jersey at the Longhorns' game against Baylor.

Thanks to Campbell and a strong defense, the Longhorns outscored their first three opponents 184–15 to move up to fifth in the AP Poll. Texas then defeated number two Oklahoma 13–6 in their annual matchup. Campbell rushed for 124 yards and scored the team's lone touchdown on a 24-yard run.

Another outstanding game from Campbell came against Texas A&M that year. He rushed for 222 yards and three touchdowns. He even added a 60-yard touchdown reception on a screen pass—the only touchdown reception of his career.

The Longhorns finished the regular season undefeated and ranked number one in both the AP and UPI polls. Texas had to beat fifth-ranked Notre Dame in the Cotton Bowl to win the national title. But Texas lost 38–10. Campbell rushed for 116 yards on 29 carries but did not score. The Notre Dame defense had three interceptions and shut down the Texas offense.

The 11–1 finish was the first of nine straight winning seasons and bowl game appearances under Akers. A strong defense lifted the 1981 Longhorns to a 10–1–1 record. They defeated third-ranked Alabama in the Cotton Bowl. The Longhorns ended the year ranked second in the AP Poll and fourth in the UPI Poll. After going 9–3 in 1982, Texas finished the 1983 regular season a perfect 11–0. The defense was outstanding once again and was led by tackle Tony Degrate.

That year the Longhorns faced number seven Georgia in the Cotton Bowl. Texas held a 9–3 lead late in the fourth quarter. But Georgia recovered a fumbled punt at the Texas 23-yard line. The Bulldogs scored with 3:22 remaining to win 10–9. Top-ranked Nebraska also lost that day. The Longhorns would have won the national championship if they had beaten Georgia.

Texas suffered key injuries in 1986 and finished just 5–6. Akers was fired after that season, despite owning a record of 86–31–2 and twice coming within one win of the national championship.

The team then turned to another former Longhorn to take control. David McWilliams was hired away from Texas Tech. He had been one of the captains on the 1963 national title team. He had also been an assistant coach for both Royal and Akers.

McWilliams produced one winning season during his first three years. But in 1990, led by sophomore quarterback Peter Gardere, the Longhorns went 10–2 and won the SWC title. The turning point in the season was a 14–13 win over number four Oklahoma.

Texas coach John Mackovic helped convince running back Ricky Williams to play for the Longhorns.

The Longhorns closed out the regular season with nine straight wins. But third-ranked Texas was blown out 46–3 by fourth-ranked Miami in the Cotton Bowl. That might have been an indication of what was to come. The Longhorns fell to 5–6 the following season and McWilliams was fired.

Unlike Akers and McWilliams, new coach John Mackovic had no previous ties to the Longhorns. But while at Texas, he recruited some of the best offensive players the program has ever known. Players such as running back Ricky Williams, quarterback James Brown, and wide receiver Mike Adams played under Mackovic.

Peter Gardere is the only Texas quarterback to beat arch-rival Oklahoma four times. He guided the Longhorns to a comeback win in 1989 as Texas beat the Sooners for the first time since 1983. Gardere rallied the Longhorns to victory again in 1990 in a 14–13 win. Texas then beat the Sooners 10–7 in 1991 and 34–24 in 1992. In his final game against the Sooners, Gardere threw for 274 yards and two touchdowns.

Mackovic's best seasons came in 1995 and 1996. The Longhorns went 10–2–1 in 1995 and won the final SWC title. The conference broke apart after the season. Texas and former SWC teams Baylor, Texas A&M, and Texas Tech merged with the teams in the Big 8 to form the new Big 12 Conference. The eighth-ranked Longhorns entered the season as one of the favorites to represent the South Division in the first Big 12 Conference Championship Game.

Texas started the season 3–4 overall and 2–2 in conference play. But behind the passing of Brown and a running game that featured sophomore Williams and senior Priest Holmes, the Longhorns won four straight games to capture the Big 12 South Division title.

The Longhorns faced number three Nebraska in the conference championship game. The two-time defending national champions were huge favorites. But the Longhorns won 37–27. Brown threw for 353 yards, and Holmes rushed for 120 yards and three touchdowns.

The key play in the game came with 2:48 remaining in the fourth quarter. The Longhorns faced fourth-and-inches at their own 28.

✕ Texas quarterback James Brown throws a pass in the team's 51–15 win over Texas A&M in 1996.

Mackovic decided to go for the first down. Instead of running the ball, Brown rolled to his left and found a wide-open Derek Lewis. He hauled in the short pass and turned it into a 61-yard play. Holmes scored on the next play to secure the upset.

That win would be the standout moment for Mackovic at Texas. The Longhorns fell to 4–7 in 1997 and Mackovic, considered an outsider by many Texas fans, was fired at the end of the season. Texas again searched for a new coach. Little did anyone know that the new coach would raise the Texas program to a level of success not seen since the retirement of Royal in 1976.

CHAPTER 5

RETURN TO GLORY

Texas continued to produce more winning seasons than losing seasons after Darrell Royal left. But it could not maintain the consistent success it experienced in the 1960s and early 1970s. That all changed when Mack Brown was hired.

Brown quickly embraced the school's rich tradition. He welcomed all former Texas players to practice. He also developed a strong relationship with Royal. Brown often asked for Royal's advice and invited him to practices.

Brown's success started in his first season. The Longhorns finished 9–3 and beat Mississippi State in the Cotton Bowl. After the SWC broke apart, the Cotton Bowl started including a Big 12 team each year. Leading the way for Texas was senior running back Ricky Williams. That season, he rushed for 2,124 yards and won the Heisman Trophy. In the regular-season finale against

Texas hired Mack Brown in 1998. The team went 9–3 that season.

WATCH RICKY RUN

Not since the days of Earl Campbell had Texas fans seen a running back as talented as Ricky Williams. He was a two-time All-American and a three-time first-team All–Big 12 selection. Williams also was the first player to win the Doak Walker Award, given to the top running back in the nation each season, twice.

Williams left Texas with 21 National Collegiate Athletic Association (NCAA) records and 46 Longhorn records to his name. His NCAA records included career rushing yards (6,279), all-purpose yards (7,206), rushing touchdowns (72), total touchdowns (75), scoring (452 points), games with a touchdown (33), and 200-yard games (11). He went on to a tumultuous career in the NFL with the Saints, Dolphins, and Ravens.

Texas A&M, Williams ran for 259 yards to become the leading rusher in NCAA history. The record-breaking yards came on a 60-yard touchdown run.

While Williams was finishing his career at Texas in 1998, quarterback Major Applewhite was starting his. Applewhite set Texas freshman records in passing yards and touchdowns in 1998. He and Williams grabbed the attention of the nation when they guided the Longhorns to a 20–16 road win over the seventh-ranked Nebraska Cornhuskers. Williams rushed for 150 yards, while Applewhite threw for 269 yards and two touchdowns.

The Longhorns had another outstanding quarterback named Chris Simms. He took over the starting role as a junior in 2001. The Longhorns rolled to a 10–1 regular season record and a berth in the Big 12 Championship Game.

✗ Texas quarterback Major Applewhite celebrates during the team's Holiday Bowl win over Washington in 2001.

The third-ranked Longhorns faced number nine Colorado. Texas was favored to win. But Colorado built a 29–10 lead in the second quarter as Simms threw three interceptions. Brown inserted Applewhite into the game, and the Longhorns immediately scored on a 79-yard pass to B. J. Johnson. But the deficit was too big to overcome. Colorado upset Texas 39–37. The loss kept the Longhorns from playing in the national championship.

Simms and sophomore running back Cedric Benson led the way in 2002. Texas finished 11–2 and beat Louisiana State University in the Cotton Bowl. Benson rushed for 1,293 yards that year. He followed that with 1,360 rushing yards in 2003.

Junior Chance Mock started the season as the top Longhorns quarterback. But freshman Vince Young was the starter by the end of the year. He threw for 1,155 yards and rushed for 998.

Texas entered the 2004 season ranked seventh. The Longhorns' only loss was a 12–0 defeat by number two Oklahoma. It was Texas's fifth straight loss to the Sooners. Oklahoma held Young to 8-for-23 passing for 86 yards. Benson gained just 92 yards rushing on 23 carries.

Texas ended the season by beating Michigan in a thrilling Rose Bowl game. Michigan took a 37–35 lead with 3:04 remaining in the game. But Young marched the Longhorns down the field. Senior kicker Dusty Mangum kicked a wobbly 37-yard field goal as time expired to give Texas the 38–37 win. Young ran for 192 yards and four touchdowns and threw for 180 yards and one touchdown in the game.

× Texas quarterback Colt McCoy throws a pass during Texas's 63–31 victory over Baylor in 2006.

The win gave the Longhorns a seven-game winning streak to end the season strong. Texas would extend that streak to 20 games by going undefeated in 2005 and beating USC 41–38 in the Rose Bowl to win the national championship.

Young decided to skip his senior season and head to the NFL in 2006. With Young gone, Texas turned to freshman Colt McCoy to be the quarterback. He struggled early in the season. But he soon proved he was capable of leading the Longhorns. Texas finished the year 10–3. McCoy threw for 2,570 yards and 29 touchdowns. Wide receiver Jordan Shipley evolved into a threat, with nine touchdown catches combined in 2006 and 2007.

The duo had a breakout season in 2008. McCoy threw for 3,859 yards and 34 touchdowns. Shipley hauled in 89 passes for 1,060 yards and 11 touchdowns as Texas went 12–1.

The team's lone loss was to number six Texas Tech. Top-ranked Texas lost 39–33 when Tech scored in the final seconds of the game. The Longhorns ended the season with a 24–21 victory over Ohio State in the Fiesta Bowl.

In 2009 only Texas Tech and Oklahoma came within 10 points of Texas during the regular season. But the Longhorns received a scare

McCOY TO SHIPLEY

From 2006 to 2009, Colt McCoy and Jordan Shipley accounted for thousands of yards on the field. McCoy set school records with 13,253 passing yards and 112 touchdowns during his career. He left Texas with a then NCAA record 45 wins as a starter.

His favorite receiver was Shipley. He ranked first in Texas history in receptions (248) and second in yards (3,191) and touchdowns (33). As a senior, Shipley set school single-season records with 116 receptions, 1,495 receiving yards, and 13 touchdown catches.

from No. 21 Nebraska in the Big 12 title game. The Cornhuskers' defense was outstanding and shut down Texas's high-powered offense. The Longhorns needed a 46-yard field goal by senior kicker Hunter Lawrence as time expired to pull out a 13–12 win and earn a berth in the national championship game against Alabama.

The game was a matchup of strengths—the Texas offense and the Alabama defense. But McCoy, who threw for 3,521 yards and 27 touchdowns that season, was knocked out of the game in the first quarter with a shoulder injury. Freshman quarterback Garrett Gilbert took over.

Alabama built a 24–6 lead at halftime. Texas rallied in the second half. Gilbert threw touchdown passes of 44 and 28 yards to Shipley to make it 24–21 with 6:15 remaining in the game. But on the Longhorns' next possession, Gilbert lost a fumble when he was sacked. Alabama scored three plays later to take a 10-point lead. Gilbert threw an interception on Texas's next drive, and Alabama scored again to win the game 37–21.

That was the last time Texas would compete for a national title under Brown. The Longhorns hadn't lost four games in a season since Brown's second year in 1999. From 2010 to 2013, they lost four in every season. Brown decided he had done all he could do for Texas and retired after the 2013 season. His 158 wins at Texas were second only to Royal.

The Longhorns knew it wouldn't be easy to replace Brown just as it hadn't been easy to replace Royal. But they thought they hired

Texas quarterback Sam Ehlinger celebrates his touchdown run against Georgia in the Longhorns' Sugar Bowl victory on January 1, 2019.

one of the best coaching candidates in the country in Charlie Strong. Strong had turned Louisville into a national contender. Certainly he could do even better at Texas.

Instead, the Longhorns got worse. Strong never posted a winning record and went to only one bowl game in three seasons. Strong was fired on November 26, 2016, one week after a loss to 1–9 Kansas, the first time Texas had lost to the Jayhawks since 1938.

Texas again hired its top choice, this time former Houston head coach Tom Herman. Coaching Texas was his dream job. He got the Longhorns back to a bowl game in 2017. Then, in 2018, Texas went 10–4, won the Sugar Bowl, and finished with a top-10 ranking.

BEVO

The Texas offensive line in the 2019 season opener weighed in at 1,505 pounds (683 kg). Those five Longhorns just edged out one real-life Longhorn on the sidelines, 1,100-pound (500-kg) Texas mascot Bevo. Bevo has had a presence at Texas home games since 1916. The fifteenth Bevo in history made his debut in 2016. A Texas student organization called the Silver Spurs cares for Bevo.

The Longhorns slipped to 8–5 in 2019, though junior quarterback Sam Ehlinger threw 32 touchdown passes. That was the second-most in team history. They ended their season on a high note with a 38–10 victory over No. 12 Utah in the Alamo Bowl. Longhorns fans hoped a return to national title contention was just around the corner.

TIMELINE

On November 30, the University of Texas defeats Dallas Football Club 18–16 in its first ever game.

1893

Texas beats rival Texas A&M 38–0 in the first game between the two schools.

1894

The undefeated Longhorns complete their perfect season by beating the undefeated Texas A&M Aggies 7–3 on November 25.

1920

In their first bowl game, the Longhorns defeat fifth-ranked Georgia Tech 14–7 in the Cotton Bowl on January 1.

1943

Number two Texas beats number one Oklahoma 28–7 on October 12.

1963

Top-ranked Texas defeats No. 2 Navy 28–6 in the Cotton Bowl on January 1. It caps off an 11–0 season that saw Texas win its first national championship.

1964

Texas defeats Alabama, crowned national champion after a perfect regular season, 21–17 in the Sugar Bowl on January 1. Ernie Koy rushes for 133 yards.

1965

Playing in the "Game of the Century" on December 6 against No. 2 Arkansas, top-ranked Texas rallies for a 15–14 victory to clinch the school's second national title.

1969

Billy Dale scores the winning touchdown as top-ranked Texas upends No. 9 Notre Dame 21–17 on January 1 to complete a perfect season.

1970

No. 1 Texas defeats No. 4 Arkansas 42–7 on December 5 to win the UPI national title for the second straight season.

1970

Ninth-ranked Notre Dame upsets number one Texas 24–11 in the Cotton Bowl on January 1 to snap the Longhorns' 30-game winning streak.

Darrell Royal coaches his final game. The Longhorns defeat Arkansas 29–12 on December 4 to send the legendary coach out with a win.

Running back Earl Campbell becomes the first Texas player to win the Heisman Trophy.

The Longhorns enter the Cotton Bowl ranked first in the country on January 1. But Notre Dame upsets Texas 38–10.

No. 2 Texas loses the Cotton Bowl on January 2, costing the Longhorns a national title.

1971

1976

1977

1978

1984

Number nine Texas beats No. 16 Texas A&M to secure the final SWC title and snap the Aggies' 31-game home winning streak on December 2.

Running back Ricky Williams races 60 yards for a touchdown against Texas A&M to become the NCAA all-time career rushing leader on November 29.

Vince Young scores the winning touchdown as the Longhorns beat USC in the Rose Bowl to clinch the national title on January 4.

Mack Brown announces his retirement from coaching Texas. His 158 wins rank second for most in school history.

Texas wins the Sugar Bowl on January 1 and ends the season ranked in the top 10 for the first time since the 2009 season.

1995

1998

2006

2013

2019

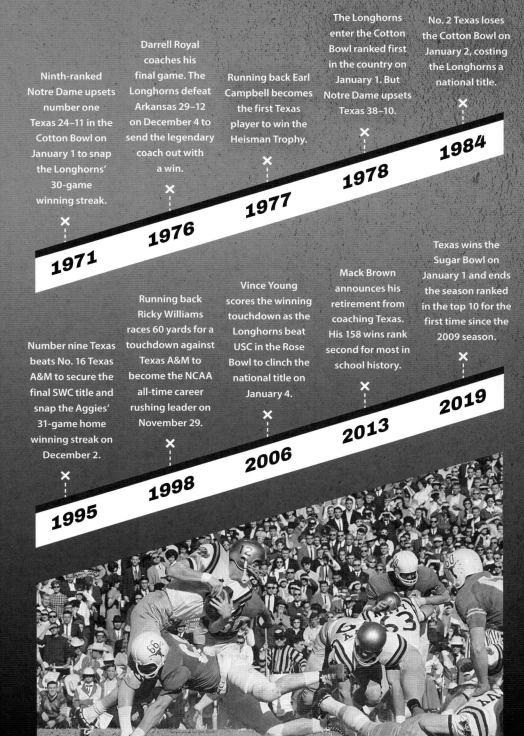

QUICK STATS

PROGRAM INFO

University of Texas Varsity
(1893–1903)
University of Texas Longhorns
(1904–)

NATIONAL CHAMPIONSHIPS

1963, 1969, 1970*, 2005

OTHER ACHIEVEMENTS

Conference titles: 32
Division titles: 7
Bowl record: 30–24–2

KEY COACHES

Dana X. Bible (1937–46)
63–31–3, 2-0-1 (bowl games)
Mack Brown (1998–2013)
158–48, 10–5 (bowl games)
Darrell Royal (1957–76)
167–47–5, 8-7-1 (bowl games)

KEY PLAYERS

Scott Appleton (OT/DT, 1961–63)
Major Applewhite (QB, 1998–2001)
Cedric Benson (RB, 2001–04)
Earl Campbell (RB, 1974–77)**
Tony Degrate (DT, 1982–84)
Peter Gardere (QB, 1989–92)
Bobby Layne (QB, 1944–47)
Colt McCoy (QB, 2006–09)
Tommy Nobis (LB/OL, 1963–65)
James Saxton (RB, 1959–61)
Jordan Shipley (WR, 2006–09)
Kenneth Sims (DT, 1978–81)
Ricky Williams (RB, 1995–98)**
Vince Young (QB, 2003–05)

HOME STADIUM

Darrell K Royal–Texas Memorial
Stadium (1924–)

*Denotes shared title
**Heisman Trophy winner
All statistics through 2019 season

QUOTES AND ANECDOTES

The Main Building, known as the tower, stands 307 feet (93.6 m) tall in the center of the University of Texas campus. During the season, the top of the tower glows orange after each football victory. Over the years, the tower has been lit entirely in orange after wins against Texas A&M, or after winning a regular season or conference title. If the Longhorns win a national title in any sport, the tower is lit entirely in orange with a "#1" displayed by turning on certain lights inside the building.

Head football coaches at Texas traditionally have ties to the program. Some played for the team during their college years and many were assistant coaches at the school. But Darrell Royal was different. He grew up in Oklahoma and later played for the rival Sooners. He learned the game from legendary Oklahoma coach Bud Wilkinson. Despite his Oklahoma roots, Royal became a Texas legend thanks to winning three national titles and never suffering a losing season in 20 years as coach.

"We couldn't do much about the negativity toward us, so we focused on the accomplishment. The satisfaction far outweighed any negativity, believe me. I'm sure the bad feelings remained nationally, but we just thought about having achieved our goals, finally."

—Texas offensive lineman David McWilliams on the Longhorns' win over Navy in 1963, weeks after the assassination of President John F. Kennedy in Dallas. Entering the game, many football fans around the country wanted Navy to win due to the events that occurred in Dallas.

GLOSSARY

All-American
Designation for players chosen as the best amateurs in the country in a particular sport.

comeback
When a team losing a game rallies to tie the score or take the lead.

conference
A group of schools that join together to create a league for their sports teams.

contender
A person or team that has a good chance at winning a championship.

deficit
The amount by which a team is trailing in a game.

draft
A system used by professional sports leagues to select new players in order to spread incoming talent among all teams. The NFL Draft is held each spring.

eluded
Avoided or got away from.

line of scrimmage
The place on the field where a play starts.

poll
A voting system in which people rank the best teams in the country.

powerhouse
A dominant team.

recruited
Convinced a high school player to attend a certain college, usually to play sports.

retire
To end one's career.

rival
An opponent with whom a player or team has a fierce and ongoing competition.

MORE
INFORMATION

BOOKS

Mason, Tyler. *The Story of the Rose Bowl*. Minneapolis, MN: Abdo Publishing, 2016.

Wilner, Barry. *The Story of the College Football National Championship Game*. Minneapolis, MN: Abdo Publishing, 2016.

York, Andy. *Ultimate College Football Road Trip*. Minneapolis, MN: Abdo Publishing, 2019.

ONLINE RESOURCES

To learn more about the Texas Longhorns, please visit **abdobooklinks.com** or scan this QR code. These links are routinely monitored and updated to provide the most current information available.

PLACES TO VISIT

College Football Hall of Fame
cfbhall.com

This hall of fame and museum in Atlanta, Georgia, highlights the greatest players and moments in the history of college football. Among the former Longhorns enshrined here are Tommy Nobis, Darrell Royal, and Earl Campbell.

The Mike Campbell–Bobby Moses Jr. Football Trophy Room
texassports.com/sports/2013/8/1/facilities_0801130827.aspx

The trophy room contains numerous awards from Longhorns history such as the 2005 national championship trophy and Earl Campbell's Heisman Trophy.

INDEX

ABOUT THE AUTHOR

William Meier has worked as an author and editor in the publishing industry for more than 25 years. He resides in St. Louis, Missouri, with his wife and their poodle, Macy.